The White House

by Jill Braithwaite

Lerner Publications Company • Minneapolis

This book is available in two editions:
Library binding by Lerner Publications Company, a division of Lerner Publishing Group
Soft cover by First Avenue Editions, an imprint of Lerner Publishing Group
241 First Avenue North
Minneapolis, MN 55401 USA

Website address: www.lernerbooks.com

Words in **bold type** are explained in a glossary on page 31.

Library of Congress Cataloging-in-Publication Data

Braithwaite, Jill.
        The White House / by Jill Braithwaite.
            p.   cm. – (Pull ahead books)
        Includes index.
        Summary: An introduction to the White House, including the history of its construction, a description of its interior and gardens, and its importance as a national symbol.
            ISBN-13: 978–0–8225–3800–4 (lib. bdg. : alk. paper)
            ISBN-10: 0–8225–3800–8 (lib. bdg. : alk. paper)
            ISBN-13: 978–0–8225–3758–8 (pbk. : alk. paper)
            ISBN-10: 0–8225–3758–3 (pbk. : alk. paper)
            1. White House (Washington, D.C.)—Juvenile literature.
        2. Washington (D.C.)—Buildings, structures, etc.—Juvenile literature. [1. White House (Washington, D.C.)
        2. Washington (D.C.)—Buildings, structures, etc.] I. Title.
        II. Series.
        F204.W5 B73 2004
        975.3–dc21   2002152402

Manufactured in the United States of America
3 4 5 6 7 8 – JR – 12 11 10 09 08 07

Who lives in this house?

The **president** of the United States
lives in this house. It is called the
White House.

The president is the leader of our country. The White House is in our nation's **capital**, Washington, D.C.

The White House is a great American **symbol**. It stands for the president and the American government.

The president and his **staff** work in the White House. Many important decisions are made there.

Leaders of other countries meet with
the president at the White House.

The president also makes speeches
from the White House.

Nearly every president has lived and worked in the White House. It has stood for more than 200 years.

President George Washington was
America's first president. He began
work on the president's house in 1792.

He chose a simple design for the house. But it still took more than eight years to build.

John Adams was the first president to live in the president's house. He and his wife, Abigail, moved there in 1800.

In 1812, the United States went to war with Great Britain. Two years later, British troops set fire to the president's house.

Workers fixed up the house after the war. They painted it white. People began calling it the White House.

Two porches were added to the White House in the 1820s. These porches are called **porticoes**. The North Portico is the main entrance.

The South Portico curves along the other side of the White House.

In 1902, the West Wing was added onto one side. The East Wing was finished in 1942.

The West Wing is an office building for the president's staff.

The president's main office is the Oval Office. Can you guess how it got its name?

The president and his family live on the second floor of the White House. This floor also has rooms for special guests.

The White House has many famous
rooms. The East Room is the largest.
Presidents hold big parties there.

Some of the rooms are named for their color. The president meets with important visitors in the Blue Room.

The Red Room is another meeting place.

Visitors can take a tour of the White House. It holds many beautiful paintings and old furniture.

The White House is sometimes called
the People's House. It belongs to all
Americans.

Maybe someday you can see the White House for yourself.

Facts about the White House

- The White House was called simply the president's house until 1901. That year, President Theodore Roosevelt officially changed the name to the White House.

- The White House is the only home of a world leader that is open for tours.

- Dolley Madison was the First Lady when the White House burned during the War of 1812. She saved a painting of George Washington from the fire. The painting still hangs in the White House. It is the only item from the original White House that remains.

- The White House has 132 rooms and 35 bathrooms. There are also 412 doors, 147 windows, 28 fireplaces, 8 staircases, and 3 elevators.

- The East Wing has a movie theater for presidents and their families. Inside the White House are also a bowling lane and a swimming pool.

The White House Gardens

President George Washington began plans for a White House Garden in 1792. Other presidents added to the garden over the years. The White House now has several different gardens.

President Thomas Jefferson planted hundreds of trees and a flower garden. President John F. Kennedy turned the Rose Garden into a place for events and speeches. The wife of President Lyndon B. Johnson began a garden just for children. Visitors can tour parts of the gardens when they come to the White House.

More about the White House

Books

Sanders, Mark. *The Presidency*. Austin, TX: Steadwell Books, 2000.

St. George, Judith. *So You Want to Be President?* New York: Philomel Books, 2000.

Barnes, Peter W. and Cheryl Shaw Barnes. *Woodrow, the White House Mouse*. New York: Scholastic, 2000.

Websites

The White House
http://www.whitehouse.gov

The White House Historical Association
http://www.whitehousehistory.org

The White House's Official Website for Kids
http://www.whitehouse.gov/kids/

Visit the White House

To plan a visit of the White House at 1600 Pennsylvania Avenue NW in Washington, D.C., you can contact one of your state's members of Congress. You can also call 202-456-7041 or go to http://www.whitehouse.gov/history/tours/ for more information. Tours are scheduled from 7:45 a.m. to 10:30 a.m. Tuesday through Saturday.

Glossary

capital: the city where the government of a country or state is located. Washington, D.C., is the capital of the United States.

porticoes: porches

president: the leader of a country, such as the United States

staff: a group of people who work for something or someone, such as the president

symbol: an object that stands for an idea, a country, or a person

Index

Photo Acknowledgments

Photographs reproduced with permission from: © William B. Folsom, pp. 3, 6, 17; © Bettmann; Stanley Tretick, 1963/CORBIS, p. 4; Photograph by Erik Kvalsvik for White House Historical Association, pp. 5, 16, 19, 27, 29; © CORBIS, p. 7; © Peter Turnley/CORBIS, p. 8; National Archives [W&C 1356], p. 9; Library of Congress, pp. 10, 11; Collection of the Maryland Historical Society, Baltimore, p. 12; National Archives, p. 13; © North Wind Picture Archives, p. 14; White House Historical Association (White House Collection), p. 15; White House Historical Association, pp. 18, 23, 24, 25; © Wally McNamee/CORBIS, p. 20; © Jack E. Boucher, The White House, p. 21; John F. Kennedy Library, p. 22; © Reuters NewMedia, Inc./CORBIS, p. 26.

Cover photo used with permission of PhotoDisc Royalty Free by Getty Images.